IN LOVE AND FAITHFULNESS

Planning for Marriage

According to the Rite of the Lutheran Book of Worship

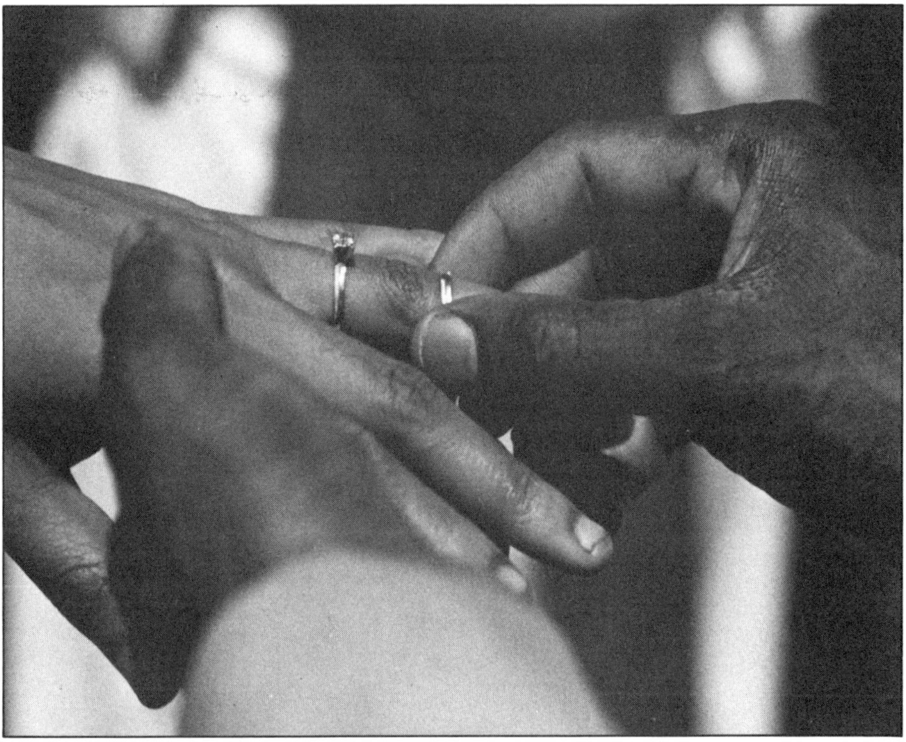

By Philip H. Pfatteicher

Edited by S. Anita Stauffer

Parish Life Press, Philadelphia

PARISH LIFE RESOURCES

This Couple's Book is accompanied by a Pastor's Guide entitled *In Love and Faithfulness: Pastor's Guide.*

Designed by Judith I. Gotwald.

Photographs by Edward A. Damerau, Jr.

Quotations from the *Lutheran Book of Worship,* copyright 1978, and the *Lutheran Book of Worship, Ministers Edition,* copyright 1978, are used by permission.

Copyright © 1982 Parish Life Press

All rights reserved. No part of this publication may be reproduced, stored in a retrieval system, or transmitted in any form or by any means, electronic, mechanical, photocopying, recording, or otherwise, without the prior permission of the copyright owner.

Printed in U.S.A.   13–900130

CONTENTS

I. Beginnings 5

II. The Marriage Service 7

Appendix 1. Outline of the Marriage Liturgy 28

Appendix 2. Worksheets........................... 29

I

BEGINNINGS

A character in Hilma Wolitzer's novel *In the Flesh* observes, "Nobody has an average marriage. You can't say that about marriage. It's a complicated relationship. Fire and ice. Passion, camaraderie, bonds of sin, love, ecstasy. It's a dangerous, even a death-defying act."[1] You are about to begin such an act.

You, who know each other only partially, plan to declare for all to hear that you will join together and share all that is to come for the rest of your lives. That bold action takes courage. Together, you are about to take a risk.

With that said, you need also to understand that marriage is God's gift to the people of his creation. God, who looked over what he had made and declared it to be "very good" (Genesis 1), made male and female for each other so that together they might reflect the image of God. Marriage, like the relationship of God to the whole world, demands a deep and lasting commitment. Together in commitment, male and female are a visible sign of the Creator's relationship to creation. God has promised that you will not be alone.

---

1. Hilma Wolitzer, *In the Flesh* (New York: William Morrow and Co., Inc., 1977), p. 188.

II

THE MARRIAGE SERVICE

Much of what the Church knows and teaches about marriage is set forth in the marriage liturgy. The marriage liturgy is therefore the most convenient and accessible place to go for a summary of what Christianity has to say about marriage. Moreover, reviewing marriage through the liturgy not only teaches you about marriage, but also helps you examine the liturgy itself to discover possible choices and variations as you shape a marriage service to suit your particular situation.

The marriage liturgy in the *Lutheran Book of Worship* has several parts:

Introduction
  Entrance
  Biblical and Theological Description of Marriage

The Marriage
  Exchange of Promises
  Exchange of Rings
  Announcement of the Marriage

Response
  Blessings
  Prayers
  Benediction

For a detailed outline of the wedding liturgy, see page 28.

MARRIAGE

BEGINNING WITH WORSHIP

A marriage is the occasion for a service of worship and praise—not just a ceremony for spectators to watch. A wedding is, first of all, a worship service. The focus is on God. That understanding of the marriage service must be clear at the outset of your planning.

The order for marriage in the *Lutheran Book of Worship* is not a rigid form. The rite is characterized by variety and flexibility, so that it may be adapted for a variety of situations. The liturgy, like marriage itself, is meant to open doors to possibilities, not to exclude creativity. As you plan your wedding, you will want to discuss the liturgical options with the pastor.

The banns of marriage are a traditional way of announcing a forthcoming marriage and inviting the prayers of the congregation for the couple. The form of the banns, as suggested in the *Lutheran Book of Worship, Ministers Edition*, may be simply, "_____*name*_____ and _____*name*_____ have announced their intention to marry on _____*date*_____, and ask your prayers." You may want to ask your pastor to read the banns or to publish them in the parish newsletter or bulletin.

In choosing the date for your wedding, avoid Holy Week, the week before Easter. During that most solemn time, all of the attention of the Church should be focused on the central events of our history—the death and resurrection of Christ. Personal celebrations detract from that solemn contemplation and are therefore inappropriate.

The marriage liturgy provides for one or more assisting ministers as well as for a presiding minister. The presiding minister is an ordained pastor who *presides* over the service. The pastor who conducts your premarital counseling normally serves as presiding minister at your marriage service. The assisting ministers may be other pastors or they may be lay persons, such as members of your families or of your wedding party. Worship is (or at least should be) a shared work of the entire congregation, and this should be evident for all to see. Persons selected to be assisting ministers should be Christians, and they should be competent in the roles assigned to them (such as reading the lessons, leading the prayers, or serving as cantor).

Stand

1. The bride, groom, and wedding party stand in front of the minister. The parents may stand behind the couple.

P The grace of our Lord Jesus Christ, the love of God, and the communion of the Holy Spirit be with you all.

C **And also with you.**

A Let us pray.

Eternal God, our creator and redeemer, as you gladdened the wedding at Cana in Galilee by the presence of your Son, so by his presence now bring your joy to this wedding. Look in favor upon _____name_____ and _____name_____ and grant that they, rejoicing in all your gifts, may at length celebrate with Christ the marriage feast which has no end. (162)

C **Amen**

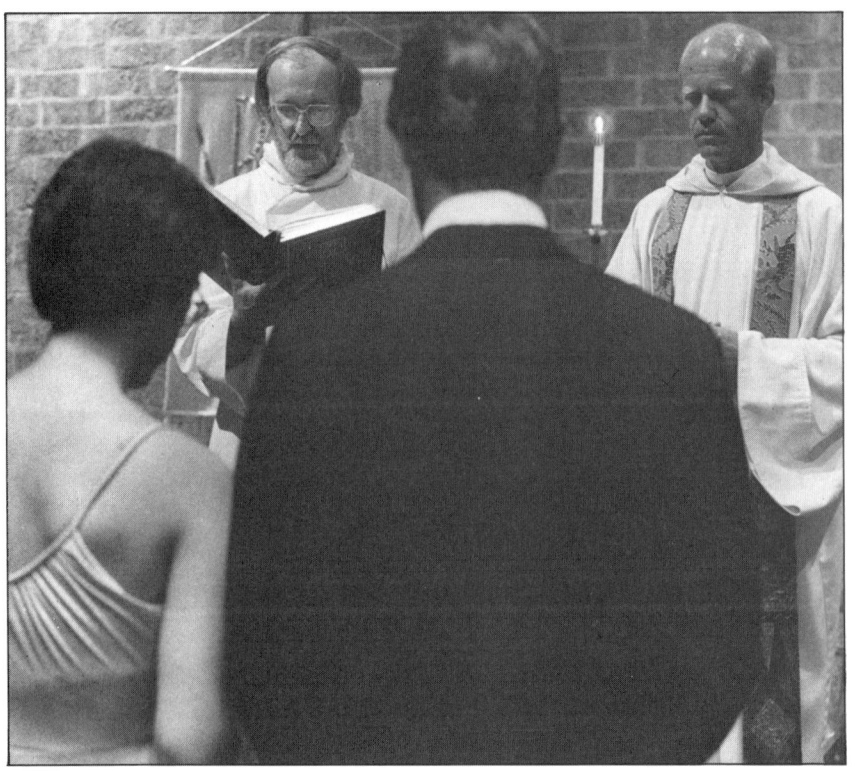

THE ENTRANCE RITE

There are many ways of entering the church and arriving in front of the presiding minister. If your wedding is small and informal, you may simply gather there (with your family and friends). Or, you may walk in procession (to music or not), coming down the aisle together behind the wedding party (if you have one) and the minister(s). Your parents may accompany you in the entrance procession to show their encouragement and support.

The Apostolic Greeting (2 Corinthians 13:14) is the same as that which begins the celebration of the Holy Communion. It sets the tone and the perspective for all that follows: Christian marriage is a service of worship of the Triune God. Grace, love, and fellowship are characteristic of the Church and of marriage. There is the intimacy within the persons of the Holy Trinity. There is the union of God with his people of all times and all places. There is the closeness of the presiding minister and the congregation as they exchange the greetings and responses. There is the union of "this man and this woman" which is about to begin. All that, and more, is suggested by these words of St. Paul.

In the Prayer of the Day ("Eternal God, our creator and redeemer . . ."), underline all the words which suggest happiness. The prayer abounds in the language of joy. Does that surprise you? God is clearly on the side of joy and gladness! That is God's will for his people; that is his intention.

The Prayer of the Day joins four events: creation with its gift of marriage (Genesis 1—2); Jesus at the wedding at Cana where he did his first miracle (John 2:1-11); your marriage; and heaven, pictured as a glad wedding banquet (Revelation 19:5-9; 21:9-14; 22:17; and Matthew 22:1-14). Old Testament and New Testament, creation and redemption, the present and the promised future are all joined—and you are part of that continuity.

Sit

2. *One or more lessons from the Bible may be read. An address may follow. A hymn may be sung.*

THE WORD OF GOD

Readings from the Bible help us understand marriage in the context of God's creative love for his people. Consider the following suggestions as you select readings for your wedding:

Genesis 1:26-31	Male and female made in God's image
Genesis 2:18-24	God creates male and female for each other
Song of Solomon 2:10-13	Love in the spring
Song of Solomon 8:7	Unquenchable love
Isaiah 63:7-9	God's love for his people
Romans 12:1-2	A living sacrifice to God
1 Corinthians 12:31—13:13	Paul's hymn to love
Ephesians 5:21-33	Marriage reflects Christ's love for the Church
Matthew 19:4-6	One flesh
John 2:1-10	Jesus at the wedding at Cana
John 15:9-12	Love one another

In addition to readings from the Bible, a selection from a secular source may be used *if it is in harmony with the spirit of a Christian service of worship and with the biblical understanding of marriage.* Be especially careful with poetry. Many love poems are personal and private expressions not appropriate for public reading at a wedding.

When a wedding takes place in the context of the Holy Communion, a Psalm is sung or said between the First and Second Lessons. This is one good way to make use of a soloist. Consider the following Psalms:

Psalm 33 A joyful song to the Creator
Psalm 100 Praise to God, the Creator and Shepherd
Psalm 117 A worldwide call to praise God
Psalm 127 Success depends on God's blessing
Psalm 128 The blessings of home
Psalm 136 Litany of praises
Psalm 150 A grand doxology

The Psalm may begin and end with one of the following Psalm antiphons:

The earth is full of the goodness of the Lord. *Psalm 33:5b*
Happy are they who delight in the commandments of the Lord. *Psalm 112:1*
They are no longer two but one. *Matthew 19:6*

A sermon may follow the readings, and a hymn may be sung. Consider the texts of the following hymns from the *Lutheran Book of Worship:*

241 We Praise You, O God
245 All People That on Earth Do Dwell
247 Holy Majesty, Before You
253 Lord Jesus Christ, Be Present Now
263 Abide with Us, Our Savior
287 O Perfect Love
288 Hear Us Now, Our God and Father
289 Heavenly Father, Hear Our Prayer
315 Love Divine, All Loves Excelling
354 Eternal God, Before Your Throne
450 Who Trusts in God a Strong Abode
451 The Lord's My Shepherd
456 The King of Love My Shepherd Is
459 O Holy Spirit, Enter In
487 Let Us Ever Walk with Jesus
507 How Firm a Foundation
512 Oh, Blest the House
529 Praise God. Praise Him
533/534 Now Thank We All Our God
551 Joyful, Joyful We Adore Thee
552 In Thee Is Gladness
557 Let All Things Now Living

A The Lord God in his goodness created us male and female, and by the gift of marriage founded human community in a joy that begins now and is brought to perfection in the life to come.

Because of sin, our age-old rebellion, the gladness of marriage can be overcast and the gift of the family can become a burden.

But because God, who established marriage, continues still to bless it with his abundant and ever-present support, we can be sustained in our weariness and have our joy restored.

JOY, SIN, JOY RESTORED

Sunlight and shadow. They are both part of life, and neither can be disregarded. In the three brief paragraphs of the assisting minister's address to the bride and groom, the Church's teaching about marriage is summarized. Two basic points are mentioned: joy and sin. In short, the joy of marriage is possible despite the fact of our sin.

Marriage, God's gift to us, shows his intention that we live in community—with him and with each other. Marriage ought to be characterized by joy—the gladness of sharing in good times and bad, the joy of finding oneself by committing oneself to another. Some of that joy is sexual. God created us male and female and saw that it was good (Genesis 1:26–31). Sex is one of God's good gifts to his creation.

Moreover, the joy of marriage is forward-looking. Our present joy points ahead in hope to the perfection of our earthly pleasure in the incomparable and indescribable bliss of heaven. As good as marriage can be, it is nothing compared to what will be in the fullness of the kingdom of God.

But human beings remain sinners who rebel against God's will and way. Sometimes the shadow of sin darkens the gladness which God intends for us, and his gifts are seen as burdens. A wife or husband, children, parents, and in-laws can become burdens as the weight of responsibility presses heavily upon us and our freedom is restricted. We cannot always do what we want. Or, by doing what we want, sometimes we avoid doing what God wants. We turn in upon ourselves in a corrupting self-centeredness. The God-willed community is broken.

Nevertheless, God's intention for joy remains, and God is always present with his abundant help—even in the midst of our rebellion. God sustains us when we grow tired and lifts us again to that joy with which marriage began.

Notice the focus of each of the three paragraphs: joy, sin, joy restored. The Lord God established marriage in joy; our self-centered sinfulness shatters it; God restores our joy. There in capsule form is salvation history. There, too, is our personal history.

[P] _____*name*_____ and _____*name*_____, if it is your intention to share with each other your joys and sorrows and all that the years will bring, with your promises bind yourselves to each other as husband and wife.

Stand

3. *The bride and groom face each other and join hands. Each, in turn, promises faithfulness to the other in these or similar words:*

I take you, _____*name*_____,
to be my *wife/husband* from this day forward,
to join with you and share all that is to come,
and I promise to be faithful to you
until death parts us.

4. *The bride and groom exchange rings with these words:*

I give you this ring as a sign of my love and faithfulness.

EXCHANGING PROMISES

If you wanted to reduce the marriage service to its simplest essential, it would be just this: the exchange of promises by the bride and groom. The heart of marriage is a promise. The entrance and the hearing of the Word of God are preparatory. Now we come to the marriage itself as you exchange your promises with each other.

The statement by the presiding minister reminds you of the function of the marriage promises: they bind you to each other for life. The pastor does not marry you; you marry each other. The pastor does not create the marriage by saying certain official words. The pastor is simply the principal witness to what you do. Marriage is your commitment to each other, shown by the promises you exchange.

As you make your promises, you face each other and join at least your right hands. (Like a handshake, it is a traditional sign of a serious commitment.) You may want to hold both hands. As indicated by the order "wife/husband" in the vow, the man traditionally says the vow first, and then the woman makes her vow. It is the promise of fidelity, not the use of a certain formula, which makes the marriage. There is nothing magic about the words themselves.

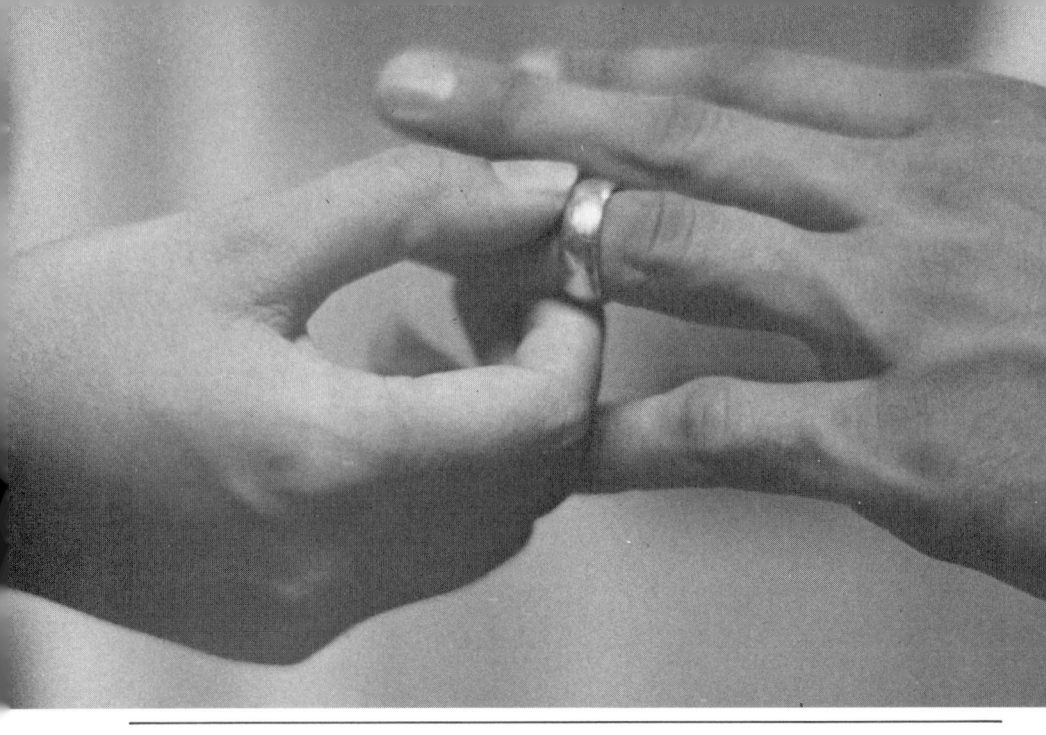

The form provided for the vow is simple and direct. There are other forms which you may want to consider; the *Ministers Edition* of the *Lutheran Book of Worship* provides three examples:

I take you, _____*name*_____, to be my wife [husband], and these things I promise you: I will be faithful to you and honest with you; I will respect, trust, help, and care for you; I will share my life with you; I will forgive you as we have been forgiven; and I will try with you better to understand ourselves, the world, and God; through the best and worst of what is to come until death parts us.

I take you, _____*name*_____, to be my wife [husband], I promise before God and these witnesses to be your faithful husband [wife], to share with you in plenty and in want, in joy and in sorrow, in sickness and in health, to forgive and strengthen you, and to join with you so that together we may serve God and others as long as we both shall live.

_____*Name*_____, I take you to be my wife [husband] from this time onward, to join with you and to share all that is to come, to give and to receive, to speak and to listen, to inspire and to respond, and in all circumstances of our life together to be loyal to you with my whole life and with all my being until death parts us.

You may wish to write your own promises. They should be consistent with the biblical understanding of marriage, and should make clear that the promises are a lifelong commitment. The pastor must approve the wording you choose if it is not a form found in the *Lutheran Book of Worship*, since it is the pastor who, as a representative of the Church, must certify that a marriage has taken place. If you write your own vows, be careful not to promise the impossible!

As a sign of the promises you have made to each other, you may exchange rings. (Sometimes only one ring is used, and there is nothing wrong with that practice if you choose it. In fact, you need not exchange rings at all.) If you do exchange rings, notice that the words which are said as the ring is given provide the title of this book. Think of the richness of both levels of meaning of "love" and "faithfulness" —ours and God's.

5. The bride and groom join hands, and the minister announces their marriage by saying:

P _____name_____ and _____name_____, by their promises before God and in the presence of this congregation, have bound themselves to one another as husband and wife.

C **Blessed be the Father and the Son and the Holy Spirit now and forever.**

P Those whom God has joined together let no one put asunder.

C **Amen**

ANNOUNCING THE MARRIAGE

Now you've done it. You are married. You have exchanged promises and signs of faithfulness to each other. So that no one will miss the significance of what has just taken place, the presiding minister announces the marriage. Notice that the announcement is in the past tense. The marriage has already taken place, and the presiding minister has been a witness to it.

The congregation responds with praise of the Triune God who has shown us the perfect pattern of love.

The presiding minister quotes Matthew 19:6, Jesus' warning against those who would tear down and destroy marriage. The words of Jesus are used here not just to silence a troublesome in-law (although that may be part of it) or a jealous friend (that may be true too), but to warn *you* that you are not to destroy what God has done in and through you. When rough times come, you must remember that marriage is more than your decision. It is also God's work. The marriage vows involve God. Yours is a triangular relationship—husband, wife, and God—and this particular love triangle is good!

By your promises you have not acted alone. The marriage is the work of God, who through your lives and the lives of others has brought you together and joined you in that state which he established at the beginning of the human race. There is more happening here than meets the eye. God works through history—through your own personal history—to accomplish his purposes for the world.

Sit

6. The bride and groom kneel.

P The Lord God, who created our first parents and established them in marriage, establish and sustain you, that you may find delight in each other and grow in holy love until your life's end.

C **Amen**

7. The parents may add their blessing with these or similar words; the wedding party may join them.

May you dwell in God's presence forever; may true and constant love preserve you.

THE BLESSINGS

The congregation, which has been standing for the central action of the marriage rite, now sits down as a way of punctuating the parts of the rite. The bride and groom (now actually the husband and wife) kneel to receive the marriage blessing.

This blessing reaches all the way back to the beginning of the human race and recalls the Lord God's creation and gift of marriage. You are in the midst of that long line of people who have been blessed by God to share in the gift of marriage.

Again, notice that the emphasis is on the delight which you are to find in each other. That is a statement of the goodwill of God and of the solidarity of the marriage promise.

Marriage is a relationship which should encourage growth. So the blessing also speaks of your growing in holy love—your love for God, your love for each other, and God's love for you. You are to show this holy love to the world more and more by the quality of your life together and by your growing and deepening relationship.

If your parents are present, and especially if they are standing close behind you, they may add their blessing. If they have been seated they may come forward at this point and lay their hands on your heads and give their blessing. The wedding party (such as the best man and the maid or matron of honor) may join them, or the wedding party may give the blessing in the absence of parents.

The blessing given in the text is from Psalm 61:7. "True and constant love" is God's kind of love, and it is also another name for God. An alternate blessing, provided by the *LBW, Ministers Edition*, is from Song of Solomon 1:4. "Let us rejoice and be glad for you; let us praise your love more than wine and your caresses more than any song."

8. The bride and groom stand.

Stand

A Let us bless God for all the gifts in which we rejoice today.

P Lord God, constant in mercy, great in faithfulness: With high praise we recall your acts of unfailing love for the human family, for the house of Israel, and for your people the Church.
We bless you for the joy which your servants, _____*name*_____ and _____*name*_____, have found in each other, and pray that you give to us such a sense of your constant love that we may employ all our strength in a life of praise of you, whose work alone holds true and endures forever. (276)

C Amen

A Let us pray for ___*name*___ and ___*name*___ in their life together.

P Faithful Lord, source of love, pour down your grace upon ___*name*___ and ___*name*___, that they may fulfill the vows they have made this day and reflect your steadfast love in their life-long faithfulness to each other. As members with them of the body of Christ, use us to support their life together; and from your great store of strength give them power and patience, affection and understanding, courage, and love toward you, toward each other, and toward the world, that they may continue together in mutual growth according to your will in Jesus Christ our Lord. (277)

C Amen

Other intercessions may be offered.

A Let us pray for all families throughout the world.

P Gracious Father, you bless the family and renew your people. Enrich husbands and wives, parents and children more and more with your grace, that, strengthening and supporting each other, they may serve those in need and be a sign of the fulfillment of your perfect kingdom, where, with your Son Jesus Christ and the Holy Spirit, you live and reign, one God through all ages of ages. (278)

C Amen

9. When Holy Communion is celebrated, the service continues with the Peace.

PRAYERS

Finally, after the marriage promises and proclamation are completed, prayers are said.

After each bid to pray (said by an assisting minister), silence may be kept while you and the congregation pray silently. Then the prayer by the presiding minister expresses the desires of the congregation.

The first prayer gives thanks for the human family, for Israel, for the Church, and for the two of you. Briefly, in a chronological survey, the sweep covers all the races of the world, the chosen people, the Church, and you. The prayer is a reminder that your lives and your marriage are lived in the context of the whole people of God. The request in the prayer is that we may not merely say our thanks but live lives of praise.

The second prayer is an intercession for you and for your lives together in communion with the Church. Although the prayer is for you, it is also for the congregation, that it may support your life together. The prayer then turns outward to the world which needs our service and ministry.

The third prayer is an intercession for all families everywhere. Those present at your wedding who are married are thus encouraged to review and renew their own marriages. The prayer asks that all marriages everywhere be more and more signs of the perfect kingdom of God where God's will is done always and joyfully.

When there is no Communion, the marriage service concludes with the prayer which Jesus taught us, which is integral to all of the services of the Church.

HOLY COMMUNION

As baptized Christians, you may request that your marriage be set in the context of the celebration of the Holy Communion.

The Holy Communion is a sign of unity, and the Sacrament is not appropriate if the congregation does not participate. The *Ministers Edition* of the *Lutheran Book of Worship* says firmly, "Under no circumstances should the bread and wine be received by the bride and groom to the exclusion of the congregation. The Sacrament is for the gathered congregation." The Communion is not exclusively yours, not even on your wedding day; the body and blood of Christ belong to the whole Church.

Celebrating marriage in the context of the Holy Communion enriches the meaning of both. Marriage often involves a festive meal; Holy Communion always does. Marriage is a sign of intimacy and union and communion; so is Holy Communion. The Holy Communion abounds in festive marriage imagery in which Christ the bridegroom celebrates with his bride the Church the heavenly wedding banquet which knows no end.

10. When there is no Communion, the service continues with the Lord's Prayer.

▣ Our Father in heaven,
    hallowed be your name,
    your kingdom come,
    your will be done,
        on earth as in heaven.
Give us today our daily bread.
Forgive us our sins
    as we forgive those
        who sin against us.
Save us from the time of trial
    and deliver us from evil.
For the kingdom, the power,
    and the glory are yours,
    now and forever. Amen
	▣ Our Father, who art in heaven,
	    hallowed be thy name,
	    thy kingdom come,
	    thy will be done,
	        on earth as it is in heaven.
	Give us this day our daily bread;
	and forgive us our trespasses,
	    as we forgive those
	        who trespass against us;
	and lead us not into temptation,
	    but deliver us from evil.
	For thine is the kingdom,
	    and the power, and the glory,
	    forever and ever. Amen

℗ Almighty God, Father, ✠ Son, and Holy Spirit, keep you in his light and truth and love now and forever.

▣ Amen

At a celebration of the Holy Communion of which marriage is a part, the Preface which the presiding minister sings or says is another clear statement of the biblical association between the steadfast love of God and the permanent commitment of the husband and wife:

> It is indeed right and salutary
> that we should at all times and in all places
> offer thanks and praise,
> O Lord, holy Father, almighty and ever-living God.
> For your love is firm as the ancient earth,
> your faithfulness fixed as the heavens.
> Creating and enriching and continuing life,
> you created us male and female
> to fulfill one another;
> you gave us the gift of marriage
> which embodies your love
> and which, even where your name is not known,
> proclaims your love for the whole human family.
> And so, with the Church on earth
> and the hosts of heaven,
> we praise your name
> and join their unending hymn.

LBW hymn 219, "Come with Us, O Blessed Jesus," is an appropriate post-Communion hymn.

The Post-Communion Prayer turns us from our own joy in this wedding to our glad service of the needy world:

Lord Jesus Christ, as you freely give yourself to your bride the Church, grant that the mystery of the union of man and woman in marriage may reveal to the world the self-giving love which you have for your Church; and to you with the Father and the Holy Spirit be glory and honor now and forever.

Marriage is for you, but you are joined to each other for the sake of others. Marriage, properly and fully understood, is a stage in moving beyond self and self-centeredness and selfishness—first to another person in self-giving love, and then in selfless service to others in the world.

Appendix 1

OUTLINE OF THE MARRIAGE LITURGY

With Holy Communion

ENTRANCE RITE

Entrance Hymn
Apostolic Greeting
Hymn of Praise: Canticle 16
Prayer of the Day

PROCLAMATION OF THE WORD

First Lesson
Psalm
Second Lesson
Verse
Gospel
Sermon
Hymn of the Day
Address by Assisting Minister

THE MARRIAGE

Exchange of Promises
Exchange of Rings
Announcement of the Marriage
Blessing by Presiding Minister
Blessing by Parents and Wedding Party
Prayers

SHARING THE EUCHARISTIC MEAL

Peace
Offering
Offertory
Offertory Prayer
Preface Dialogue
Proper Preface for Marriage
Prayer of Thanksgiving and Lord's Prayer
Communion
Post-Communion Blessing
Post-Communion Canticle or Hymn
Post-Communion Prayer
Blessing
Dismissal

As a Separate Service

ENTRANCE RITE

Hymn or Instrumental Music
Apostolic Greeting

Prayer of the Day

PROCLAMATION OF THE WORD

Lesson(s)

Sermon
Hymn
Address by Assisting Minister

THE MARRIAGE

Exchange of Promises
Exchange of Rings
Announcement of the Marriage
Blessing by Presiding Minister
Blessing by Parents and Wedding Party
Prayers
Lord's Prayer
Blessing

Appendix 2

WORKSHEETS

WEDDING INFORMATION FOR PASTOR

Bride's Name: _____
  Address: _____
  Phone: _____
  Date of Birth: _____
  Place of Birth: _____
  Date of Baptism: _____
  Place of Baptism: _____
  Congregation: _____

Groom's Name: _____
  Address: _____
  Phone: _____
  Date of Birth: _____
  Place of Birth: _____
  Date of Baptism: _____
  Place of Baptism: _____
  Congregation: _____

Maid or Matron of Honor: _____
Bridesmaids: _____
_____
_____
_____

Best Man: _____
Ushers: _____
_____
_____
_____

CHECKLIST FOR PLANNING

To be completed with the pastor

Wedding Date: _____
    Time: _____
    Place: _____
Rehearsal Date: _____
    Time: _____
Presiding Minister: _____
Assisting Minister(s): _____
Organist: _____
Other Musician(s): _____
Will Holy Communion be celebrated? _____
Prelude: _____
Entrance Music: _____
Hymn: _____
Concluding Music: _____
Lesson(s): _____
    Lector(s): _____
Text of Marriage Vow:

One ring or two? _____
Will parents and/or the wedding party give the blessing? _____
    Text:

Which translation of the Lord's Prayer will be used? _____

If Holy Communion Is Celebrated

Who will sing Canticle 16 as the Hymn of Praise (congregation, choir, or soloist)?
_____

First Lesson: _____
   Lector: _____
Psalm: _____
   Sung by: _____
Second Lesson: _____
   Lector: _____
Verse to be sung by: _____
Gospel: _____
   Lector: _____
Hymn of the Day: _____
Will the Peace be shared by the congregation? _____
Will an offering of money be received? _____
   If so, what will be done with the money? _____
Who will provide the bread? _____
Who will provide the wine? _____
Who will present the bread and wine? _____
Who will be the assisting minister for the distribution? _____
_____
_____